The Rathmines Stylebook

David Rice

The writing guidelines used in the Rathmines School of Journalism

Folens

To my Mother, whose children's stories charmed our childhood

Editor: *Rachel O'Connor*

Lay-out & Design: *Teresa Burke*

The cover for this book was designed and produced on the computerised pagemaking system of the Rathmines School of Journalism, using 3B2 software. The cover photo is an Ektachrome transparency from the School of Journalism's photo library. It shows the clocktower of Rathmines, with Rathmines Road in the foreground and the Dublin mountains in the background. It was taken with a Nikon 400mm ED telephoto lens.
Cover design and photo © by David Rice.

ISBN: 0 86121 4382

Originally for private circulation within the Rathmines School of Journalism. First general release, 1993.

Copyright © 1982, 1987, 1992, 1993, by David Rice. All rights reserved.

Folens Publishers, Airton Road, Tallaght, Dublin 24.

Contents

Foreword

The College of Commerce has been a major provider of journalism education since the 1960s. Generations of students have graduated from the College and are now professional journalists in all areas of the media, in Ireland and throughout the world.

This stylebook, devised by David Rice, seeks to codify practices which have developed over the years on the Rathmines journalism course, and which are based on widely-accepted newspaper practice.

The College is pleased, through David's book, to share its experience with all involved in journalism. We also hope that it will be useful generally in the education system, in particular in the developed courses designed to introduce students to writing, and to the world of the media.

James S. Hickey
Director
College of Commerce, Rathmines
Dublin Institute of Technology

A word from Douglas Gageby

We are writing to be understood, and this book will help.
Keep it simple and short, and you can't go far wrong.
And when you've written it, re-read and see if it couldn't be even simpler: better still, ask someone else to read it for you. Or read it out aloud to yourself.
It's no good if there is room for any doubt as to the meaning of even one sentence.
Avoid fashionable formulae. When will we be rid of "state-of-the-art"?
And, when in doubt, refer to *The Rathmines Stylebook.*

Douglas Gageby
(formerly editor of *The Irish Times* and extern
examiner to the Rathmines School of Journalism)

What is The Rathmines Stylebook?

Do you write **alright** or **all right**? Should you write **okay** or **OK**? Is it correct to write **11 A.M.**? Or should you write **11 AM, 11 a.m., 11 o'clock**, or **eleven o'clock**? Do you say **the Government is** or **the Government are**? Or does it matter which?

Which is more correct – **a fifteen year old girl**, or **a fifteen-year-old girl**, or a **15-year-old girl**? Or should you even write **girl** at all? Perhaps 15-year-olds would prefer to be called **young women**? And if so, should their wishes be respected?

Should you write **A.I.D.S.**, or **AIDS**, or **Aids**? Should you write **seven percent**, **7 percent**, **7 per cent**, **7%**, or **7 p.c.**? And if you saw all five versions together in a newspaper article, would it irritate you? Should **R.T.E.** have those full stops between the letters, or should it be **RTE**?

Or does it matter a hoot?

Yes, it does. For unless your writing is consistent and disciplined, readers get irritated. And editors get mad.

But where can you get guidance? Grammar books are no help, because this is not a matter of grammar – most of the above examples are grammatically correct.

And that's what *The Rathmines Stylebook* is about. It ventures beyond grammar and syntax, into that jungle where there are no rules – rules about whether to write **Miss, Ms.,** or **Ms** – and simply decides on one of the options.

But the decisions are far from arbitrary. Newspapers over the years have evolved their own consistent styles, and, more than 12 years ago, at the Rathmines School of Journalism, I introduced a stylebook I had developed that was meant to reflect the general usage throughout Ireland.

Its aim was that our journalism graduates should have a disciplined style, and fit easily into any newsroom in the country. It gradually became known as *The Rathmines Stylebook*.

The word "stylebook" is really a misnomer. It is not about "stylish" writing, nor is it about "political correctness". It is about writing with clarity and consistency, and about referring to individuals and groups with respect and sensitivity. In other words, aiming for excellence.

The Rathmines Stylebook was meant only for private circulation to our students and graduates. But we have been overwhelmed with requests for copies, from newspaper offices, public relations firms, advertising agencies, universities, and third-level colleges – indeed anywhere writing is done. And now more and more secondary schools are asking for copies.

So we have agreed finally to share this little book with everyone. *The Rathmines Stylebook* is now being published for the first time.

I hope you find it helpful.

A heartfelt thanks to Frances O'Rourke, Features Editor of the *Sunday Press*, John Brophy of the *Irish Press*, Pat Stacey of the *Irish Independent*, and to my colleague, Desmond Fennell, who scrutinised a most complicated text, and made so many constructive suggestions.

David Rice
The Rathmines School of Journalism*
Dublin Institute of Technology
September 1993

* "The Rathmines School of Journalism" is the name popularly given to the journalism course run by the Dublin Institute of Technology.

A

Abbreviations

> **Basic Rule**: Abbreviations confuse people. Use them only when absolutely clear and familiar to readers. In doubt, spell them out in first reference.

The following can be abbreviated:

- Personal titles and courtesy titles (**Mr**, **Mrs**, **Prof**, **Cllr**, etc). See under "Courtesy Titles" for full details.

- In full numbered addresses, **Street**, **Road**, **Avenue**, **Terrace** can be shortened to **St**, **Rd**, **Ave**, **Tce** –

   He lived at 42 Tullow St.

- Generic words in business titles, when they *end* the title –

   Irish Ropes plc
   Irish Sugar Co (but **Company Printers Ltd**)
   O'Dea & Co
   Time Inc (but **Incorporated Law Society**)
   General Motors Corp

Note: Certain words are customarily not abbreviated: **society**, **association**, **group**, **institute** –

   Irish Distillers Group
   Bank Officials' Association
   Irish Farmers' Association
   Irish Cancer Society

- Measure words (**oz, lb, st, in, ft, yd, mm, cm, m, km, cc, mph, mpg**) when they follow a figure. Eg –

  He was 5 ft 4 in tall.

See also under "Capitals" and "Numbers".

- The ampersand (**&**) may be used in company title. Eg –

  P&O Line
  B&I Line (no longer **B+I**)
  O'Dea & Co

Plc can usually be omitted from ordinary news reports.

- Degrees are abbreviated without full points (**BA**, **MA**, **PhD**, **MSc**). Prefer **HDE** to **H. Dip. Ed.**, which is unwieldy without full points. Note that news reports rarely require degrees after a name. When one does, it is better to say –

  Ms Smith, who has a master's degree
  from Trinity and a Higher Diploma in
  Education from Galway, ...

Note the apostrophe after **master's** and **bachelor's**.

- The **Co** in names of counties (**Co Down**): otherwise **county** is spelt out. Eg –

  The county manager says that
  Co Longford must ...

- **Junior,** after a name, is shortened to **Jr**, not **Jnr**.

See also under "Acronyms".

Absolutes/superlatives

Absolutes/superlatives should be avoided. Beware absolutes like –

Everyone agrees that ...
It is axiomatic that ...
A unique example of ...
The only woman ever to ...

Someone is sure to disagree.

Likewise beware of superlatives (**the biggest, the best, the first**). *The Guinness Book of Records* made its money on the fact that someone always claims another biggest, best or first. Avoid even –

The last surviving veteran of the Boer War ...

Those veterans are lurking everywhere, waiting to pounce on the unsuspecting absolute or superlative.

At least qualify the statement or attribute it to someone –

One of the biggest ...
Among the last surviving veterans ...
What its architects claim to be the
tallest building ...

Accents

Irish and foreign words should be written with their accents.
Exception: Irish words that have become a part of English – eg, **Gardai**, **Dail** – may be written without accents.
Note: The **O'** in certain names is sometimes written **Ó** even in English versions of a name. Observe name-bearer's preference.

See also under "Gaelic names"; "Irish-language words".

Acronyms/initial clusters

For difference between acronyms and initial clusters, check glossary at end of book.

Basic Rule 1: Avoid acronyms and initial clusters especially on first reference, unless thoroughly familiar to readers.

They are better avoided even on second reference too. Where unavoidable, follow this rule –

- First reference: Spell it out in full, but do not put initials in brackets after it. So do not say –

The Teachers' Union of Ireland (TUI) ...

- Second reference: Simply use the initials. Thus –

Members of the Teachers' Union of Ireland are to go on strike from Monday. A bulletin issued at the TUI headquarters ...

However, it is just as easy to say –

A bulletin issued at the union's headquarters ...

thus eliminating the initial cluster.

Note: Just occasionally it can make for easier reading to use initial cluster at start of story. But it should be spelt out in full as soon as possible later in the story.

Basic Rule 2: Omit all full points with acronyms and initial clusters.

Exceptions to this rule: **a.m.**, **p.m.** Also a person's initials get full points (**Mr J.J. Smith**).

In headlines a greater flexibility is allowed in the use of acronyms and initial clusters, but the above-stated cautions remain.

A small number of initial clusters and acronyms have become familiar to readers. These can be excepted from the basic rule and used in first reference.
Here are some familiar initial clusters –

AD	FCA	ITV	PD	RIP	UFO
a.m.	FM	JCB	PESP	RTE	UN
AWOL	GAA	JP	plc	RUC	US
BA	GMT	KGB	PhD	SC	USA
BBC	GPO	LW	PLO	SOS	UTV
BC	HIV	MA	p.m.	SS	UVF
BL	HQ	MEP	PMPA	TCD	VEC
CIA	IBM	MI5	PR	TD	VD
DCU	IFA	MP	PRO	TV	VHF
DIT	INLA	MSc	PRSI	UCC	VHI
DIY	INTO	MW	PS	UCD	VIP
EC	IOU	NCO	PVC	UCG	YMCA
ESB	IQ	PAYE	QE2	UDA	YWCA
FBI	IRA	PC	RC	UDR	

Initial clusters are written *all capitals* (with a few exceptions such as **a.m., p.m., plc, PhD, MSc**).

Note: If your software and printing system has *small caps**, prefer them for initial clusters. They make the initial cluster less obtrusive (eg, **John Smith**, FRCSI, rather than **John Smith, FRCSI**). But this is a fine point.

* (For meaning of *small caps*, see glossary at end of book.)

And here are some familiar acronyms (Note: Acronyms are not written in capitals but like ordinary words) –

Acot	**Fás**	**laser**	**Siptu**	**Unicef**
Aids	**Gatt**	**Nato**	**Spuc**	**Unifil**
Cert	**Gestapo**	**radar**	**Unesco**	**Usit**

Addresses

> **Basic Rule**: Full addresses, including house numbers, are required in court reporting. Otherwise addresses should be provided where relevant to the story.

Amount of address-information required is relative to a paper's circulation area. Thus a national paper might report –

> **A father of 15 drowned last night**
> **when ...**

Whereas that story might appear in a Carlow paper as –

> **Mr John Smith, of 42 Tullow Street,**
> **Carlow, drowned last night when ...**

Note: The sub-editor may choose to omit the house number, to prevent intimidation or hate mail.

In full numbered addresses, **Street, Road, Avenue,** and **Terrace** can be abbreviated to **St, Rd, Ave, Tce** –

> **He lived at 42 Tullow St.**
> but
> **Tullow Street is being dug up.**

When a house has a name instead of a street number, do not place the name in quotes. Thus –

The Laurels
not
"The Laurels"

A complete postal address is presented thus –

**Mrs Mary Smith, 35 Rathmines Rd,
Dublin 6. Tel. (01) 970666**

Note that commas set off each section, except for the full stop before the telephone number.

Streets are lower case in plural. Thus –

O'Connell and Grafton streets
not
O'Connell and Grafton Streets

Admit

Avoid this word. It can suggest a previous attempt to conceal some fact.

Aeroplane

Aeroplane or **plane**, not **airplane**. But prefer specific words – **an Aer Lingus Boeing 737; Israeli jets; a British Airways jumbo; airliner; corporate jet; bomber; fighter; light plane; US strike aircraft.**
Note: **Aircraft** is best used collectively (as in **Shorts, the aircraft manufacturers**).

Age

A person's age should be included if relevant to the story. Otherwise omit it.

It is taken to be relevant in reference to persons taken into custody or appearing on criminal charges in court.

It is frequently deemed relevant when someone –
- dies; or
- is involved in an accident; or
- is a child; or
- is the victim of a crime (especially when elderly).

Style for expressing age –

> **An eight-year-old child was …**
> **Mr Murphy, who was 63, had been …**
> **John Smith, 26, of no fixed address …**

Note that age is placed between commas, not in brackets.

Words to describe age should be selected, not just with precision, but with sensitivity. The following guide is based partly on Associated Press practice (but modifed for Irish needs):

Infant: Up to 12 months.
Child: Up to 10 years.
Boy: Up to 14th birthday (after which say **young man**, or **man**).
Girl: Up to 14th birthday (after which say **young woman**, or **woman**).

Note: Thus cut-off point was suggested by members of the Rathmines journalism class.

Youth: Between 13 and 18 years. Generally used only for males.
As noun, can have negative connotations –

> **Three youths were taken into custody …**

Youngster: Up to about 15 years (mostly used in feature writing). Eg –

They were charming youngsters.

Teenager: Up to about 15 years.

Young people: Between 15 and 25 years.

Middle-aged: Caution. Bear in mind *Chambers's Dictionary* definition of middle age as "between youth and age, variously reckoned to suit the reckoner". The term is better avoided. Thus –

Gardai are looking for a man in his
early 50s ...

Elderly, old, aged: Same caution here. Certainly never for under 70. Best used generically. Eg –

A home for the elderly ...
Problems of old people ...

Note: Anyone under 16 involved in a court case (in any role) must not be identified, directly or indirectly.

See also under "Numbers".

Air Corps

Say **the Air Corps,** not **the Irish Air Corps**.

Ranks as in the Army, except –

Rank	*First reference*	*Second reference*
Flight Sergeant	**Flight Sgt John Smith**	**Fls Smith**
Flight Sergeant-Major	**Flight Sgt-Maj John Smith**	**FSM Smith**

All right

All right is right. **Alright** is not.

Alleged

Alleged indicates that an action is not proven, and that you are not presenting it as fact. Story must include the source of the allegation.

Note: Use of **alleged** does not protect against action for libel.

Alternative

Alternative means one of two. When more than two, say **options** or **choices** –

> **He had three options** (not **alternatives**).
> **A whole range of choices**

Ampersand

Ampersand (&) should be used in company titles. Eg –

> **P&O**
> **O'Dea & Co**
> **B&I Line**

Do not use it in headlines. In fact **and** should be avoided in headlines whenever possible, as its only acceptable abbreviation seems to be the grotesque comma –

> **Wet, dry spells expected**

Army ranks

The Army Press Office was consulted for the following usage. However, we have made slight modifications for this stylebook, eliminating less familiar terms like **COS**, **ACS**, **2 Lt**, etc, and also eliminating full points.

Rank	*First reference*	*Second reference*
Private	**Pte John Smith**	**Pte Smith**
Corporal	**Cpl John Smith**	**Cpl Smith**
Sergeant	**Sgt John Smith**	**Sgt Smith**
Company Quartermaster-Sergeant	**CQMS John Smith**	**CQMS Smith**
Company Sergeant	**CS John Smith**	**CS Smith**
Battalion Quartermaster-Sergeant	**BQMS John Smith**	**BQMS Smith**
Sergeant-Major	**SM John Smith**	**SM Smith**
Battalion Sergeant-Major	**BSM John Smith**	**BSM Smith**
Regimental Sergeant-Major	**RSM John Smith**	**RSM Smith**
Second Lieutenant	**2nd Lt John Smith**	**Lt Smith**
Lieutenant	**Lt John Smith**	**Lt Smith**

Rank	First reference	Second reference
Captain	**Capt John Smith**	**Capt Smith**
Commandant	**Comdt John Smith**	**Comdt Smith**
Lieutenant-Colonel	**Lt-Col John Smith**	**Lt-Col Smith**
Colonel	**Col John Smith**	**Col Smith**
Brigadier-General	**Brig-Gen John Smith**	**Gen Smith**
Adjutant-General	**Adjutant-Gen John Smith**	**Gen Smith**
Quartermaster-General	**Quartermaster-Gen John Smith**	**Gen Smith**
Major-General	**Major-Gen John Smith**	**Maj-Gen Smith**
Lieutenant-General	**Lt-Gen John Smith**	**Lt-Gen Smith**

Note 1: Spell out all other military functions, even on second reference, except **OC** (Officer Commanding) and **GOC** (General Officer Commanding). Do not write **O/C**.

Note 2: Do not say **the Irish Army**: say **the Army**. For armies of other countries, put **army** in lower case (**the French army**).

Average

Avoid the statistical terms **mean, median** and **mode**, where possible, except in technical writing. Prefer words like **average** and **normal**.

Note: In a range of annual temperatures, for a particular date, of 3, 10, 14, 22, 22 –

- **Averag**e or **mean** temperature is 14.8. You add all the figures, and divide by their number.
- **Normal** temperature is 22. It is the most frequently occurring figure. Also called the **norm** or **mode**.
- **Median** temperature is 14. It is the figure in the middle, when the figures are arranged from lowest to highest.

B

Bible

Bible should be capitalised. Likewise **Koran**, **Book of Mormon**, and the sacred books of any faith. Do not capitalise adjectives derived from them: **biblical**, **koranic**.

Biblical names: Take the spelling from the *Revised Standard Version*, which is common to Protestants and Catholics.

Bible references: Put book number first (**2 Kings** for **the Second Book of Kings**), then chapter number followed by verse number, all in arabic figures, and separated by commas. Thus –

> **2 Kings, 4, 12**
> **Matthew, 25, 37-38**
> **1 Cor, 13, 4 - 5**

Billion

Billion is a thousand million (not a million million, as formerly). Can be abbreviated to **bn**, if it occurs frequently in a story –

£8.5 bn in promised EC funding ...

Bitch

Bitch, not **lady dog**, or **female dog**.

Blonde

Blonde is a woman with **blond** hair.

Book references

Style is as follows –

> **Hodgson, F.W.** *Modern Newspaper Practice.*
> **London: William Heinemann, 1987.**
> **Price £8.95.**

Note: If a book price is available only in sterling, do not translate into punts, but put **in Britain** after the figure.

Brackets

Brackets **( )** should not contain a full stop, unless they contain a full sentence *which is completely independent.* Eg –

> **He loves his country (Ireland).**
> **He loves his country (it is Ireland).**
> but
> **He loves his country. (We love people, not countries.)**

Note: Brackets are also called *parentheses*; what they contain is a *parenthesis*.
See also under "Square brackets".

Brand names/trade names

Avoid. See under "Capitals".

British terms

Certain British terms, political and geographical, could upset readers in the Republic, and should be avoided. Besides, some of them can be inaccurate when used here. Avoid these –

> **Mainland Britain**
> **The United Kingdom** (say **Britain**)
> **The Queen** (say **Queen Elizabeth**)
> **The Prime Minister** (say **Britain's prime minister**
>   or **British Prime Minister John Smith**)
> **The British Isles** (say **Britain and Ireland**)
> **Ulster** (when referring to Northern Ireland)
> **The Six Counties**
> **The Cabinet** (say **the British cabinet**)
> **The Government** (say **the British government**)
> **Londonderry** (say **Derry**)
> **Eire** (say **Ireland**)

Note: **UK** should not be used even as an adjective. Use **British** instead.

C

Capitals

> **Basic Rule**: Use lower case unless there is a clear reason for using a capital letter.

Capitalise these –

- First word of a sentence.

- Proper nouns, when used in first full reference. Thus –

> **Arriving at St John's Church, he found the church empty.**
>
> **Galway County Council is requiring members of the council to ...**

- Months; days of the week (**April; Tuesday**). But not seasons (**spring**).

- Official titles (**President Robinson**). But note that mere roles or functions which are not titles are in lower case, and follow the name (**John Smith, the referee ...**).

If in doubt whether a function is also a title, give benefit of doubt and capitalise.

- Principal words in titles of creative works, such as books, plays, songs. Capitalise all except prepositions, conjunctions and articles (definite and indefinite). Eg –

  Finnegans Wake
  The Plough and the Stars
  The Yellow Submarine
  Portrait of the Artist as a Young Man

- Names of streets. But word **street** is lower case in plural. Eg –

  O'Connell Street
  but
  O'Connell and Grafton streets

- Official names of associations, companies, organisations, institutions, political parties, etc. Eg –

  University of Dublin
  Belgard Heights Residents' Association

- Brand names; trade names (**Coke**; **Bic**, **Benzedrine**; **Formica**; **Caterpillar**; **JCB**; **Vaseline**; **Sellotape,** etc).

Use a trade name only if it is essential to the story: otherwise prefer generic words (**cola**; **ballpoint**; **stimulant**; **plastic covering**; **earthmoving equipment**; **petroleum jelly**; **sticky tape**, etc). Note that some companies employ press-cutting services to monitor the use of their trade names, and take vigorous action when such trade names appear in lower case.

- **The President.**

- **The Taoiseach.**

- **The Government** (when referring to **the Irish Government**).

- **The Army**, **the Air Corps**, **the Naval Service** (in reference to Irish services).

- Geographical terms widely accepted (**Middle East**; **the Orient**; **the North**; **the Golden Vale**; **the West**). But compass-points are lower case (**the wind is from the west**).

- The **The** in **The Irish Times** and **The Times**. These newspapers have the definite article as part of their title. Compare with **the Irish Independent**; **the Evening Press**.

- Names of political parties –

    The Democratic Unionists
    The Communist Party

    But not adjectives or common nouns –

    Several unionist viewpoints . . .
    There was communist influence . . .

    There are no communists in the Democratic Party and there are no democrats in the Communist Party.

- Most abbreviations (**Mr, Prof**, etc). But see below for exceptions such as **p.m.**

- **God**, and words referring to the Deity in all religions (**Allah**; **Jehovah**; **Jahweh**). Also all pronouns and possessive adjectives referring to God and Jesus –

    Hallowed be Thy Name
    Our Father Who art in Heaven

- Battles and wars –

   The Battle of Kinsale
   World War II

- Sacred books (**the Bible; the Koran; the Gospels**).
   But lower case when used as adjective (**biblical**).

- Churches; recognised religious denominations –

   The Free Presbyterians
   The Catholic Church

- Church members and religious adjectives –

   She is a Catholic and her husband is a Protestant.

   A Protestant school and a Jewish synagogue

- Religious services and feast days of all denominations –

   Mass
   Evensong
   Pentecost
   Bar Mitzvah
   Passover

- Leadership titles, when used as proper nouns –

   The Taoiseach met the Bishop of Cork.

   The Ayatollah has offered a reward.
   but
   A former taoiseach says he wants to
   become a bishop or an ayatollah.

- **General election**, when specific –

  > **The General Election of 1987 is only
  > one of several general elections ...**

- **County**, when specific –

  > **Co Cork is the largest county.**

- **Garda**, referring to the force. But a single **garda** is lower case. Eg –

  > **A Garda spokesman said ...**
  > but
  > **A garda came on the scene.**

  See under "Garda Siochana ranks" for more details.

- **The High Court**, but **a high-court case**. Likewise for other courts.

Do not capitalise these (unless they begin a sentence) –

- The following abbreviations: **a.m.**, **p.m.**, **eg, etc**, **ie**, **viz**, **agm**, **adm**, **plc** (note that **a.m.** and **p.m.** take full points).

- Abbreviations of measure words: **oz, lb, st, in, ft, yd, mm, cm, m, km, cc, mph, mpg.**

  See also under "Numbers".

- Animal types (**terrier**; **collie**; **hereford**; **jersey**; even **rhode island red** and **german shepherd**). But the **Irish** in **Irish terrier** takes a capital, since lower-case **i** would look odd.

- **de Valera**; **de Gaulle**; **von Gallen**; **di Maggio**; and other foreign names beginning with particles, unless they start a sentence. Irish names like **ffrench** and **d'Arcy** depend on family usage, and must be individually noted.

  Note: Eamon De Valera of the *Irish Press* prefers a capital **De**.

- Seasons of the year (**spring; autumn**).

- Proper names in plural –

  > **Christ Church and St Patrick's cathedrals**
  > **The Supreme and High courts**
  > **O'Connell and Grafton streets**

- Derivatives of proper names *now become common nouns* (**dutch treat; brussels sprouts; french fries; roman numerals; plaster of paris; dutch courage; scotch whisky; manhattan cocktail; venetian blind.**
  But **Irish coffee** and **Irish stew** get a capital, as lower-case **i** looks awkward.

- Compass points (**north; east; northeast**).

- Titles when used as common nouns –

  > **There were three cardinals and two bishops.**
  > **A US president once said …**
  > **The words of a pope**
  > but
  > **The words of the Pope**

- Foreign governments. Eg –

  British government sources ...
  The French government ...

- Irish past governments. Eg –

  the Haughey government
  but
  the Irish Government

Catchline

Catchline is a single word, selected by the writer, that serves to identify the story at all stages of writing, editing, headline writing and typesetting.

Put it at the top right-hand corner of every page of the story (it serves the same function as a name tag on the wrist of a newly-born baby – hopefully preventing mix-ups).

Try to select a word that clearly identifies your story and avoids confusion with any other story. So avoid words like **accident**, as there may be several accidents that day. Other words to avoid are –

minister	**court**	**sport**
taoiseach	**crime**	**woman**
murder	**disaster**	**child**
fire	**man**	**judge**

Above all, avoid the word **kill**, as that word instructs the compositors to discard the story.

See also "Copy preparation".

Catholic Church titles

Most church titles have been considerably simplified in newspapers during the last few years. The following is broadly acceptable today –

Title	First reference	Second reference
Diocesan priest	**Rev John Smith**	**Fr Smith**
Parish priest	**Very Rev John Smith**	**Fr Smith**
Religious order priest	**Father John Smith**	**Fr Smith**
Brother	**Brother John Smith**	**Br Smith**
Sister	**Sister Frances Smith**	**Sr Frances** or **Sr Smith** (depending on order's usage)
Male religious superior	**Very Rev John Smith**	**Fr Smith**
Female religious superior	**Mother Frances Smith**	**Mother Frances** or **Mother Smith** (depending on order's usage)
Monsignor	**Msgr John Smith**	**Msgr Smith**
Canon	**Canon John Smith**	**Canon Smith** or **the Canon**
Archdeacon	**Archdeacon John Smith**	**Archdeacon Smith** or **the Archdeacon**

Bishop	**The Bishop of Ossory, Dr Smith** or **Bishop Smith of Ossory**	**Dr Smith** or **Bishop Smith**
Archbishop	**The Archbishop of Dublin, Dr Smith** or **Archbishop Smith of Dublin**	**Dr Smith** or **Archbishop Smith** or **the Archbishop**
Cardinal	**Cardinal Smith** (not **John Cardinal Smith**)	**Cardinal Smith** or **the Cardinal**
Pope	**Pope John Paul II**	**the Pope** or **Pope John Paul** or **the Pontiff**

Note: A priest-member of a religious order gets title **Father**, not **Rev**, on first reference (unless he is a superior). See above.
See also "Clerical titles" ; "Nuns/sisters"; "Religious orders".

Chinese names

The *pinyin* method of rendering Chinese in Latin script has been universally adopted by the news agencies, replacing the older Wade-Giles method. Also all place names have been standardised in Mandarin. The principal changes you will encounter are geographic. **Peking** becomes **Beijing**; **Canton** becomes **Guandong**. **Nanking** becomes **Nanjing**.

Mao T'se Tung becomes **Mao Zedong**. **Chou En Lai** becomes **Zhou Enlai**. **Teng Hsiao Ping** becomes **Deng Xiaoping**.

Christian name

The christian or first name must always be given in first reference. Initials are not usually sufficient, unless the person is normally called by initials (see under "Names").

Christian or first names should never be abbreviated (**Ml**, **Jos**, **Jn**). Nor should short forms be used unless it is the person's preferred style (eg, **Jack Charlton**; **Jimmy Carter**; **Jim Kemmy**; **Sammy Davis, Jr**).

Church of Ireland titles

Title	*First reference*	*Second reference*
Deacon, Minister or Priest	**Rev John Smith**	**Mr Smith** (but see note 1 below)
Woman Priest	**Rev Jane Smith**	**Mrs/Miss/Ms Smith**
Canon	**Canon John Smith**	**Canon Smith**
Archdeacon	**The Archdeacon of Cashel, Ven John Smith** or **Archdeacon Smith of Cashel**	**Archdeacon Smith** or the Archdeacon
Dean	**The Dean of Cashel, Very Rev John Smith** or **Dean Smith of Cashel**	**Dean Smith** or **the Dean**
Bishop	**The Bishop of Cloyne, Rt Rev John Smith** or **Bishop Smith of Cloyne**	**The Bishop** or **Bishop Smith**
Archbishop	**The Archbishop of Dublin, Most Rev John Smith** or **Archbishop Smith of Dublin**	**The Archbishop** or **Archbishop Smith**

Note 1: Some Anglican priests prefer the title **Father**.
Note 2: Church of Ireland bishops use the title **Dr** only when they hold a doctorate.
Note 3: The Bishop of Meath always has the title **Most Rev**.

Claim

Avoid this word, unless you wish to cast doubt on what is reported (eg, **He claimed to be innocent**). Instead, use **say** or **said**.

Clerical titles

For specifics see under the following entries: "Catholic Church titles"; "Church of Ireland titles"; "Jewish titles"; "Methodist Church titles"; "Presbyterian Church titles"; "Religious Orders" .

The following are general guidelines:

When a priest or minister has a doctorate, the title **Dr** supercedes **Fr** or **Mr**.
Catholic bishops and archbishops and the Chief Rabbi, take the courtesy title, **Dr**. Church of Ireland bishops do not (unless they hold a doctorate).

It is not necessary to say **the Church of Ireland Archbishop of Dublin**, or **the Roman Catholic Archbishop of Dublin**. Simply say **the Archbishop of Dublin**, and let the name and context indicate which denomination is intended.

Clichés

Clichés are phrases that have been so overworked as to have lost almost all meaning. The Rathmines School of Journalism is instituting an annual *Hee-Haw Award* for the year's dumbest and most overworked utterance. Trophy is a Braying Donkey, cast in bronze. Candidates for the award, at the time of writing, are –

> **on the back burner**
> **copperfasten**
> **level playingfield**
> **at this point in time**
> **upmarket**
> **at the coalface**
> **at the cutting edge**
> **linkage**
> **window of opportunity**
> **in the pipeline**
> **war-torn**
> **at grassroots level**
> **the bottom line**
> **as of yet**
> **ride roughshod**
> **unmitigated disaster**
> **in the frame**
> **radical concept**
> **interface**
> **state of the art**
> **full employment the No. 1 priority**

We would welcome proposals for further candidates for the award.

Basic rule: Avoid clichés and jargon like the plague (that's a cliché), except in reported speech. And avoid even then, if possible.

c.o.d.

c.o.d. is always lower case, and retains the full points. Means "cash on delivery".

Collective nouns

Collective nouns take singular verbs. Thus –

> **The Government is planning ...**
> **The jury has considered its verdict**
> **Dublin Corporation has announced ...**
> **A herd of cattle has stampeded ...**

Exceptions: Teams are considered plural in sports reports, and pop music groups usually take the plural. Thus –

> **Donegal captured their first All-Ireland ...**
> **U2 are planning another world tour ...**

Note: **Garda** (the force) takes the singular, whereas **the Gardai** (a group of individual officers) takes the plural. Thus –

> **The Garda is reorganising**
> but
> **The Gardai have arrived on the scene.**

See also under "Garda Siochana ranks".

Colon

Colon (:) is used as follows:

1. Between two complete sentences, when one flows from the other. Eg –

> **He turned back: there was really no choice.**

2. To introduce a list of items. Eg –

   Three people came: Peter, James, and John.

3. To introduce a quoted sentence. Eg–

   He said: "The judge does not believe her."

   But <u>not</u> before an incomplete sentence–

   He said he "did not believe her".

Note: in 1 and 2 above, a dash (–) can be used instead of a colon. Eg –

   He turned back – there was really no choice.

   Three people came – Peter, James, and John.

Comma

Use as follows:

1. To mark a natural pause in the writing.

2. To avoid ambiguity, so the reader does not have to go over the sentence twice. Eg –

   On the balcony above, a man gazed, a
   woman holding his hand ...

Without the commas this could read –

   On the balcony above a man
   gazed a woman
   holding his hand [presumably
   reaching down to do so!].

3. In a series –

> **Green, white, and orange** (Note: Put comma before the **and**).

4. Between adjectives –
> **a grey, bleak, windy day**

5. Before or after a quote –

> **He said, "You are the only one in my life."**
> **"I love you," he said.**

Note: before longer quotes, a colon may be used. See under "Colon".

6. To take the place of brackets or dashes. Eg –

> **This man (whom I love) is dying.**

It is simpler to write –

> **This man, whom I love, is dying.**

Note 1: You cannot use one of these commas without the other.
Note 2: If the **whom I love** phrase is essential to identify the man, DO NOT USE COMMAS. Thus –

> **The man whom I love is dying** (ie, no other one is dying).

Whereas with commas the sense is: The man is dying – maybe others are too – and I love him.

Note 3: In the above example (Note 2) you could replace **whom** by **that** –

The man that I love is dying.

(although some editors still restrict **that** to non-persons).

But NB: it is preferable to omit **that** altogether –

The man I love is dying.

Comprise / compose / consist / constitute

Use as follows –

Ireland comprises 32 counties.
Ireland is composed of 32 counties.
Ireland consists of 32 counties.
Thirty-two counties constitute Ireland.

NB: Never write **is comprised of.**

Copy presentation

Most periodicals have particular requirements on how they want stories presented. However, the following are minimum requirements, applicable to word processors and typewriters:

- Use white A4-size paper (ie, double the size of this page).

- Type one side of page only. Double space, and set the word-processor or typewriter at 60 spaces across each line (this gives an average 10 words to a line, which helps in estimating story length). One way to do this is to set left margin at 20 and the right margin at 80.

- Do not indent first paragraph. Indent all other paragraphs five spaces (unless instructed otherwise).

- Skip a line between each paragraph.

- Never run a paragraph from one page to another.

- Keep paragraphs short.

- At the top right-hand corner of *every* page put the following:
  Catchline *
  Your name or initials
  Page number

(* See glossary for what a *catchline* is. See also entry "Catchline".)

- Put the word **more**, or **MF** (= **more follows**), at bottom right-hand corner of every page but the last.

On first page:
Add the date under the catchline, etc.

Start the story halfway down the first page. If you have a provisional feature title, put it immediately above the story at this point on the page.

On middle pages:
Start about three inches from top of each page.

On last page:
As middle pages, but put **ends** immediately after the final paragraph, centred on the page.

Freelances often attach a cover page to the whole lot, giving title of feature, full name and address and telephone number of writer, the rights offered, and any copyright details.

Note: Modern computerised editorial departments may set different guidelines – eg, may not require indented paragraphs. Check with editors where possible.

Courtesy titles

Courtesy titles (**Mr, Mrs, Miss, Ms**) are used without full points –

> **Mr John Smith**
> **Mrs Jean Smith**

Courtesy titles are customarily omitted for persons charged with criminal offenses, or arrested in connection with them –

> **Appearing on a charge of assault was**
> **John Smith ...**

They are often omitted for people in show-business, for sports persons, celebrities, politicians, accident victims –

> **Among the injured were John Smith**
> **and Frank Murphy of ...**
> **Elizabeth Taylor is to marry again.**

If a title appears before the name, courtesy title can be omitted –

> **IFA President John Smith**

Miss, **Mrs** are used according to a person's marital status. But if a married woman uses her maiden name, use courtesy title **Miss**.

Ms is used in two cases only: (1) when marital status is unknown; (2) when the person has indicated a preference for **Ms**.

Dr is used for physicians and holders of university doctorates (except honorary ones). But surgeons (FRCSI) prefer the title **Mr** or **Ms**.

See also under "Medical titles".

One who holds a chair at university, medical school, or hospital, gets the title **Prof**.

Esq has no place in newspaper style.

*Note: A growing number of newspapers are dispensing altogether with the courtesy title **Mr** on first reference. We strongly recommend this.*

See also entry on "Names", which should be read in conjunction with this entry.

D

Dash

The dash (–) – also called the *en rule* – can be used as follows:

1. To take the place of brackets. Eg –

> **There are many good reasons – this is one – why he should go.**

2. To take the place of a colon. Eg –

> **There was only one outcome – death.**

Note: The dash is often preferable to brackets or colon, as it is less formal.

3. To indicate a sudden change in thought. Eg –

> **I will go if I am well enough – a very
> big IF, I regret to say.**

Note: If word-processor lacks special key for dash, use two hyphens, with space before and after. Likewise for typewriter.

Date

> **Basic Rule:** When writing dates, put month first, then day and year –

> **June 12, 1988**
> **Feb. 16 – 28, 1995**

Omit **th** after day-numeral (so, <u>not</u> **June 12th**). Put comma between day-numeral and year .

Spell out the name of the month. So never write **6/12/1988**, as it could be read as Dec. 6 instead of June 12.

When an event will occur, or has occurred, within the year, it is not necessary to write the year –

> **He died in January.**
> **Competition closes Aug. 31.**

In full dates, the Associated Press recommends abbreviating the following months (with full point) –

Jan.
Feb.
Aug.
Sept.
Oct.
Nov.
Dec.

The others are spelt in full. Thus –

April 30, 1988
but
Feb. 28, 1973

These abbreviations are only for dates. Otherwise months are spelt out in full –

August is a wicked month.

Other dates are expressed thus –

The class of '83 (use apostrophe)
Back in the 1880s (no apostrophe)
300 BC
AD 432
The ninth century
The 20th century

In dates, a hyphen cannot be substituted for the word **to** –

The 1988–89 school year
but
The school year runs from 1988 to 1989.
(Do not write **from 1988–89**)

Widely-accepted phrases should be spelt out –

**The Gay Twenties
The culture of the Sixties**

Day

Spell days in full, and capitalise –

**The death took place on Monday
(**not **Mon.) ...**

Use **today**, **late last night**, **yesterday**, **early this morning**, etc, as appropriate to time of newspaper publication.

Note: **Today** is not hyphenated.

ALWAYS include the actual day in brackets, as an aid to the sub-editor. It is the sub's role to delete this before sending for setting –

**A father of four died early this
morning (Friday) when his car went
off the road ...**

It is rarely necessary to say **next Monday** or **last Monday**. Within seven days before or after event, use of future or past tense provides all necessary information –

**The parade will take place on Monday
at noon (**not **next Monday at noon**:
it's obviously next Monday).

The death occurred on Monday (it's
obviously last Monday).

Rarely does the insertion of **next** or **last** add anything to the information.

Outside of seven days before or after publication, use both day and date –

> **The parade takes place on Monday,**
> **July 12, and ...**

See also entries "Date" and "Time".

Degrees

Degrees take no full points (**BA, MSc, PhD**). Note: It is often unnecessary to put the degrees after a person's name. When a degree is relevant to the story, write thus –

> **Ms Smith, who holds a master's**
> **degree from Trinity, ...**

Note the possessive apostrophe in **master's**.

Prefer **HDE** to the cumbersome **H. Dip. Ed**. which can hardly survive without full points.

Note: Degrees are conferred: people are not. So do not write **was conferred with a degree**. Write **a degree was conferred on**.

Derogatory words

Derogatory words should not be used, except in reported speech.

Note that certain words, even if once acceptable, are now derogatory, or at least unacceptable to the individual or group designated.

Basic Rule: Members of most groups have one preferred word to denote themselves. Find the word they prefer, and use it.

Here are some of these preferred words –

Traveller (not **knacker**, **tinker** or even **itinerant**)
Woman (not **lady**)
Muslim (not **Moslem** or **Mohammedan**)
Protestant (not **non-catholic**)
Catholic (not **RC**)
Black or **Afro-American** (not **negro**, or **coloured**)
Scots or **Scottish** (not **Scotch**)
Disabled (not **handicapped**, or **crippled**)
Gay or **homosexual** (not **homo**)
Latin American (not **South American**)
Married priest or **resigned priest** (not **ex-priest**)
Students (not **pupils**, or **children**)
Young woman (not **girl**)
Young man (not **youth**, or **boy**)
Saudi Arabian (not **Arab**)
Algerian (not **Arab**) (likewise for other North African nationalities)
African (not **negro**, or **coloured**)
Native American (not **Red Indian**)
Chinese (not **Chinaman**)
Japanese (not **Jap**)
Inuit (not **Eskimo**)
British (not **Brit**)
Prison officer (not **warder**)

Disc

As in compact discs, insurance discs, parking discs.

Disk

As in computers.

E / F

EC

EC, not **EEC**.

Elderly

See note under "Age".

English / British

English refers to the people and things of England. **British** refers to England, Scotland and Wales together. Therefore say **British government, British soldiers** (not **English government, English soldiers**).

Exclamation mark (!)

Avoid, except in quoting direct speech, and even then use sparingly.

Fiancé / fiancée

Fiancé is the man; **Fiancée** is the woman.

Foreign language words

Foreign language words are to be avoided where possible. When used, they should be italic (unless they have become part of the English language, eg, **blitz**, **de facto**, **de luxe**, **fiancée**), with accents as required. If typewriter or software does not support the *umlaut* (¨) in German words, add an E after the vowel. Eg – **Führer** becomes **Fuehrer**.

Irish language words are not considered foreign, so do not take italics. They do, however, require accents, unless they have also become part of everyday English. Eg – **Gardai; Dail.**

Four-letter words / obscenities

Avoid, except in reported speech – and then only if it is essential to the story.
Note: It is preferable to use an obscenity, or avoid it altogether, than to pussyfoot around it with expressions like **He told her to "f--k off"**.

Fractions

Change to decimals where possible. Eg –

$$2\,{}^{3}/_{4} \text{ becomes } \mathbf{2.75}$$
$$2\,{}^{1}/_{4} \text{ becomes } \mathbf{2.25}$$

Further / farther

Further refers to time (**He worked further into the night**). **Farther** implies distance (**He drove farther into the mountains**).

G

Gaelic names

In all cases follow name-bearer's preference.

Masculine **Ó** takes an accent.

Mac, never **Mc**

If masculine surname starts with **h**, the **h** is usually lower case, and the following vowel is capital (**Ó hÓra**; **Ó hÉalaí**).

The feminine **Ní** takes **h** after the initial consonant (**Ní Mhurcú**). If the initial is a vowel, the **h** goes first (**Caitlín Ní hUallacháin**).

The surname **Breathnach** is, unlike most others, an adjective. It therefore takes **h** in the feminine (**Niamh Bhreathnach**).

Note: Gaelic surnames are names in their own right. Therefore when a person uses a Gaelic name, it should not be translated into English.

Garda Siochana ranks

Rank	*First reference*	*Second reference*
Garda	**Garda John Smith**	**Garda Smith**
Detective-Garda	**Det-Garda John Smith**	**Det-Garda Smith**
Detective-Sergeant	**Det-Sergeant John Smith**	**Det-Sgt Smith**
Detective-Inspector	**Det-Inspector John Smith**	**Det-Inspector Smith**
Superintendent	**Supt John Smith**	**Supt Smith** or **the Superintendent**
Chief Superintendent	**Chief Supt John Smith**	**Chief Supt Smith** or **the Chief Superintendent**
Assistant Commissioner	**Asst Commissioner John Smith**	**Asst Commissioner Smith** or **the Assistant Commissioner**
Deputy Commissioner	**Deputy Commissioner John Smith**	**Deputy Commissioner Smith** or **the Deputy Commissioner**
Commissioner	**The Garda Commissioner, Mr Smith**	**Commissioner Smith** or **Mr Smith** or **the Commissioner**

Note 1: **Detective-Garda** is the same rank as **Garda**. The term **Detective** merely denotes a (plain-clothes) function which the individual is carrying out within the rank he holds. Likewise for **Detective-Sergeant** and **Detective-Inspector**. Thus it is inaccurate to

say that an individual has been "demoted" from detective-garda rank to that of garda.

Note 2: The RUC equivalent to commissioner rank is that of **Chief Constable**.

Note 3: **The Garda** refers to the force itself and takes a singular verb –

The Garda is planning to ...

The Gardai means the officers themselves, and takes a plural verb –

The Gardai are patrolling O'Connell Street.

Note 4: **Garda** is capitalised (1) when it is the force; (2) when it is a title –

Garda John Smith

It is lower-case when it refers to an individual, unnamed officer –

A garda came on the scene.

In plural, it is lower- case when used without **the** –

Two gardai arrived.

but

The Gardai were summoned.

Note 5: The term **Ban Garda** has been discarded. Say **Garda**.

Gender-free expressions

When the subject could be male or female, avoid sentences that force you to say **he** or **his.** Eg –

A journalist should use his head.

Instead, use the plural, which is gender free –

> **Journalists should use their heads.**

Do not use any of the following –

> **One should use one's head.**
> or
> **A journalist should use his or her head.**
> or
> **A journalist should use his/her head.**

See also under "Sexist Language".

Gentleman

Avoid. Prefer **man**.

Government

Government is capitalised when it is the Irish Government. Say **the Government**, not **the Irish Government**.

See also under "Public life titles".

H

Headlines

Headlines are exempt from many of the basic rules of the stylebook (because of the need for brevity), but not from the need to have a subject and a verb (at least implied) in most cases.

Historic

Write **a historic occasion**, not **an historic occasion**.

Hope

Avoid **it is hoped** and **hopefully**. Eg, do not say –

> **Hopefully sales will increase.**
> or
> **It is hoped to increase sales.**

Instead, say something like –

> **The manager hopes to increase sales.**

Hotel

Write **a hotel**, not **an hotel**.

Hyphen

Basic Rule 1: Use hyphen whenever it helps to avoid confusion or ambiguity. Thus –

> **He recovered the armchair** (it had
> been stolen).
> but
> **He re-covered the armchair** (the
> covering was threadbare).

Basic Rule 2: Use hyphen to form one adjective from two or more words. Thus –

> **The half-time score**
> **Day-to-day living**
> **A well-known author**

Use hyphen to avoid double vowels or triple consonants –

> **anti-intellectual**
> **co-operate**
> **bell-like**

Numerals: Hyphenate **twenty-one** to **ninety-nine**, in the rare cases when these must be spelt out (eg, when starting a sentence).

Many word combinations that are not hyphenated must carry a hyphen if they *precede* a noun (this is Rule 2 in another guise) –

> **He lived from day to day.** But **Day-to-day living**
> **Have a good time.** But **Good-time Charlie**
> **He was rarely seen.** But **The rarely-seen man**
> **She is 10 years old.** But **A 10-year-old girl**
> **He drank after hours.** But **after-hours drinking**

Distinguish *hyphen* (-) and *dash* (–). To get typesetter to set dash (ie, en-rule), type hyphen twice on copy, with space before and after.

Note: Word processors sometimes have a special key for dash.

Suspensive hyphen is used thus –

> **The judge imposed a 25- to 30-year sentence.**

However, suspensive hyphenation is clumsy and better avoided.

Hypothetical condition

Use **were**, not **was**. Eg –

> **If I was at home right now ...** (quite possible)
> but
> **If I were a rich man ...** (hypothetical)

I

Initial clusters

See under "Acronyms/initial clusters", and "Names".

Insertions into quotes

Insertions into a quote should be in square brackets, if available to typesetters. Otherwise use round brackets –

> **"I love this country [Ireland] more
> than any other," he said.**

Ireland

Ireland is the political term for the 26-county Republic of Ireland *(as defined in the Constitution)*. It is also the geographical term for the whole 32-county island.

Do not write **Éire**, unless you are writing in Irish.

Irish-language words

Irish-language words are written with their accents, and do not take italics.

Exception: Words that have become part of everyday English – such as **Gardai, Dail** – can dispense with the accent.

Italics

Use them for titles of magazines, newspapers, books, plays, ballets, operas. Also for symphonies and concertos, but only if they have a particular name. Eg –

Beethoven: Piano Concerto
No. 5 in E flat *Emperor*

Use double quotes for arias within an opera. For recorded pop music, use italics for albums and double quotes for the individual tracks. Use neither italics nor quotes for the name of a pop group.

Note: If word processor or typewriter lacks italics, underline the word. If it lacks bold type, and you want the word in bold, underline, but write the word **bold** in a circle beside it.

Its / it's

Its is the possessive of **it**. **It's** means **it is** or **it has**. Eg –

The dog bit its owner, so it's going to be
put down. It's got to be done.

J

Jail

Jail, not **gaol**.

Jewish titles

Title	*First reference*	*Second reference*
Rabbi	**Rabbi John Smith**	**Rabbi Smith** or **the Rabbi**
Chief Rabbi of Ireland	**The Chief Rabbi, Dr Mirvis**	**Dr Mirvis** or **the Chief Rabbi**

Note: The Chief Rabbi should be given the courtesy title **Dr**, as is given to bishops and archbishops.

Judgment

Judgment, not **judgement**.

L

Lady

Avoid. Prefer **woman** or **female.** But note that **lady** is still sometimes used in stories relating to sport (**Ladies' Day**; **Lady Captain**).

Also avoid **lady dog** or **female dog**. Say **bitch**.

Legal profession titles

Role	First reference	Second reference
District Court Justice	**District Justice Smith**	**Judge Smith** or **the Judge** or **the District Justice**
Circuit Criminal / Civil Court Judge	**Judge Smith**	**Judge Smith** or **the Judge**
High Court Judge	**Mr Justice Smith** (or **Mrs/Miss/Ms**)	**The Judge** or **Mr Justice Smith**
Central Criminal Court Judge	**Mr Justice Smith** (or **Mrs/Miss/Ms**)	**The Judge** or **Mr Justice Smith**
Supreme Court Judge	**Mr Justice Smith** (or **Mrs/Miss/Ms**)	**The Judge** or **Mr Justice Smith**
Circuit Court President	**The President of the Circuit Court, Mr Justice Smith** (or **Mrs/Miss/Ms**)	**The President** or **the Judge** or **Mr Justice Smith**
High Court President	**The President of the High Court, Mr Justice Smith** (or **Mrs/Miss/Ms**)	**The President** or **the Judge** or **Mr Justice Smith**
Chief Justice	**The Chief Justice, Mr Justice Smith** (or **Mrs/Miss/Ms**)	**The Chief Justice** or **Mr Justice Smith**
Barrister	**Mr John Smith, BL (for Jones)**, …	**Mr Smith** or **counsel for the plantiff / defendant / accused**

Role	*First reference*	*Second reference*
Senior Counsel	**Mr John Smith, SC, counsel for the plaintiff / defendant / accused**	**Mr Smith** or **counsel for the plaintiff / defendant / accused** or **Jones's counsel**

Note 1: In criminal cases the accused does not get the courtesy title, **Mr, Mrs, Miss, Ms**. In civil cases both defendant and plaintiff get the title –

> **John Smith admitted assaulting Mr Jim Jones on Oct. 8. Smith had been ...**
> but
> **Mr Jim Jones said that Mr Smith had promised him ...**

Note 2: Plural of **counsel** is **counsel.**

Listings

Newspaper diary listings (music, theatre, etc) allow much more abbreviation than elsewhere. So discard stylebook niceties here and go for brevity, *provided clarity is maintained.*

When writing listings, model them on the previous day's entries. Note that style varies considerably from paper to paper.

M

Medical / hospital titles

Graduates of medical school have the title **Dr**.

Surgeons (fellows of Royal College of Surgeons or similar body) take title **Mr** or **Ms**. In first reference the name is followed by the appropriate letters, such as **FRCSI**.

However obstetricians and gynaecologists, even when surgeons, are customarily called **Dr**.

A medical person with a chair in university, medical school, or hospital, takes the title **Prof**.

A nurse in hospital management, including Director of Nursing (formerly Matron), has the title **Mrs**, **Miss**, **Ms**, or **Mr**.

Female nurse in charge of ward has title **Sister**. Male nurse in charge of ward is called **Mr**.

Staff nurses, both senior and junior, are referred to as **Staff Nurse**.

A student or undergraduate nurse is referred to as **Nurse**.

Methodist Church titles

Title	*First reference*	*Second reference*
Minister	**Rev John Smith**	**Mr Smith**
President	**Rev John Smith, President of the Methodist Church in Ircland**	**Mr Smith**
Bishop	Note: Although the Methodist churches have bishops, there are none in the Methodist Church in Ireland.	

See also entry, "Clerical titles."

Middle names

(Eg, John **Francis** Smith) should be used where identification is crucial – as in names of those accused of crime, or of those involved in a disaster such as an air crash.

Money

Punts: Express thus: **£4.25**; **£3,000**; **80p**; **5p**; **£20.50**; **£20** (not **£20.00**).

Write **Irish pound** rather than **punt**.

Do not write **IR£** unless context requires it.

Sterling: Convert it into Irish pounds where possible. Otherwise write **stg** after the figure –

The fare is £80 stg.

Million: Spell the word out (do not use **M** or **m**) –

The Government owes £300 million.

Billion: As million –

£33 billion in arms expenditure ...

But note: In a story with frequent reference to **million** or **billion**, the abbreviations **m** and **bn** are acceptable. They are also acceptable in headlines.

Foreign currencies: Spell them out, except dollars and Deutschmarks (the symbols for which are widely known). Eg –

He was paid $3,000 and DM 5,000.
but
The cost was 200 French francs.

Mr, Mrs, Miss, Ms

See under "Courtesy Titles."

N

Names

Names make friends; errors make enemies. Absolute accuracy in the spelling of personal names is essential, even if it means painstaking and prolonged checking.

Use of christian or first name:

> **Basic Rule:** On first reference, first name must be given. On second reference, omit first name –

> **Mr John Smith, president of the Irish Farmers' Association, died last night. Mr Smith, who was 48, …**

> **Mrs Jeanne Smith has resigned as director of the Well Woman Centre. Mrs Smith had been ill for some time …**

Exceptions: Certain titles in public life, law titles and clerical titles, do not require first name on first reference (see under "Legal Profession", etc) –

> **The Taoiseach, Mr Smith**
> **Mr Justice Smith**
> **The Archbishop of Dublin, Dr Smith**

Initials are not an adequate substitute for a person's first name (on first reference). So **Mr J. Smith** is unacceptable.

Exceptions: For some people, initials have taken the place of the first name, and thus are adequate on first reference. Eg –

> **P.P. O'Reilly**
> **B.P. Fallon**
> **Dr A.J.F. O'Reilly**
> **W.B. Yeats**

This is often the preferred style for active and retired rugby players.

Note that such initials take full points, even though the accompanying courtesy title (**Mr** or **Dr**) does not.

A married woman is referred to by her own first name, not that of her husband. Thus –

Mrs Mary Smith (not **Mrs John Smith**)

When writing of couples, say –

John and Mary Smith
(not Mr and Mrs John Smith)

Note: In society listings, you can write **the John and Mary Smiths**.

In criminal cases include the middle names of accused persons, to minimise danger of confusion with other persons. Thus –

John Francis Xavier Smith was given
a 12-month suspended sentence ...

Likewise when listing victims of disasters.

Note: **O'** becomes **Ó** in Gaelic, and sometimes remains so even in the English form. Follow name-bearer's preference.

See also under "Gaelic names".

Nato / NATO

Nato means the North Atlantic Treaty Organisation, and has become a word in its own right (ie, an acronym).

NATO is the National Association of Tenants' Organisations, and is spelt out in first reference.

Naval Service ranks

Rank	First reference	Second reference
Ordinary Seaman	**OS John Smith**	**OS Smith**
Able Seaman	**AS John Smith**	**AS Smith**
Leading Seaman	**LS John Smith**	**LS Smith**
Petty Officer	**PO John Smith**	**PO Smith**
Chief Petty Officer	**CPO John Smith**	**CPO Smith**
Warrant Officer	**WO John Smith**	**WO Smith**
Ensign	**Ens John Smith**	**Ens Smith**
Sub-Lieutenant	**S-Lt John Smith (NS)**	**S-Lt Smith**
Lieutenant	**Lt John Smith (NS)**	**Lt Smith**
Commander	**Cdr John Smith**	**Cdr Smith**
Captain	**Capt John Smith (NS)**	**Capt Smith**
Commodore	**Comdr John Smith**	**Comdr Smith**

Note 1: Where Naval Service ranks resemble those of the Army, **NS** should be put in brackets after the name (meaning **Naval Service**).

Note 2: Say **the Naval Service**, not **the Irish Naval Service**.

No one

No one, not **no-one**.

Northern Ireland

Northern Ireland is the political term for the six-county region ruled from London. It can also be called **the North**. **Ulster** refers to the nine-county province.

Numbers

> **Basic Rule**: Spell out cardinal numbers from **one** to **nine**. From **10** on, use figures –

There were five men and 12 women ...

Same for ordinal numbers: spell out **first** to **ninth**; from **10th** on, use figures. Do not put full point after the **th** –

He played the Fifth Symphony for the 10th time.

Exceptions to the above rule:

Use only figures for the following (even **1** to **9**) – sums of money; addresses; measurements, including distance, height, weight, volume, temperature, speed. Also use figures for dates; sports scores; voting results; and after the abbreviation **No.** (which is followed by a full point) –

9 Myrtle Park, Swords, Co Dublin
Try room No. 3
Tickets cost £5 each

Do not start a sentence with a numeral. If, however, the context forces you to do so, then spell out the numeral (even when **10** and above) –

Thirty-two people died when their bus crashed ...

Exception: A year can start a sentence, and remain in figures –

1982 was a good year for wine.

Spell out conversational phrases, such as –

A hundred thousand welcomes
Thanks a million
The Gay Nineties

Use roman numerals for monarchs, wars, popes –

Pope John XXIII
World War II
Richard III

Roman numerals are as follows –

I = 1	**C** = 100
V = 5	**D** = 500
X = 10	**M** = 1000
L = 50	

Form other roman numerals thus:
When a letter *follows* another of same or greater value, add the values (eg, **VI** = 5 + 1 = 6). When a letter *precedes* another letter of greater value, subtract the former (eg, **IV** = 5 - 1 = 4). So **1987** is **MCMLXXXVII**, and **1994** is **MCMXCIV**.

Note: To get the roman numeral **I**, type a capital **i**, not the figure **1**.

Use figures, not roman numerals, for **RTE 1**; **Network 2**; **BBC 1** and **2**; **FM 3**; **Channel 4**.

Use comma when figures exceeds three digits, except in dates –

1,000
250,550
but
1994

Million: In money, use figures, but spell out the word **million** immediately after the figure. In all other cases follow basic rule for numerals (above) –

> **The Government owes £300 million.**
> **Six million Jews died in World War II.**
> **There are 1,200 million people in China.**

Billion follows same rules.

See also note under "Money", for when **million** and **billion** can be abbreviated.

Fractions should be translated into decimals where possible, rounding to second decimal place. So **13$^3/_4$** becomes **13.75**; **5$^1/_4$ million** becomes **5.25 million**.

Measurements use only figures, and lower-case abbreviations in the singular. They are presented thus –

Speed: **His speed was 65 mph.**

Temperature: **Temperature is 20° C, 68° F.**
                       Temperature is minus 10° C.
                       (spell out **minus** – do not use a hyphen)

Weight: **The baby weighed 7 lb 4 oz.**
                       A 15st man
                       A haul of 5 kg of cocaine

Length / Height: **He is 5 ft 4 in tall.**
                       A 300ft drop
                       A 35mm camera

Distance:	**The 25yd line**
	A 100m dash
	5 yd, 2 ft, 4 in
	25 km
	10 m, 8.4 cm
Area/capacity:	**Office space at £50 per sq ft**
	An area of 40 sq in
	It contained 50 cc
	A 500cc Honda motorcycle

Note 1: When the measurement serves as an adjective, there is no space between figure and measure word. Eg –

> **The 5ft man**
> but
> **He is 5 ft tall.**

Note 2: Attitudes to metric and imperial measures are still fluid. Follow the popular preference in whatever category of measurement you are dealing with. These preferences are indicated in the above listing.

Percentages: write **15 per cent** (not **15 percent**; **15 pc**, or **15%**).
Use only figures, even from **1** to **9**. But note that financial reporting has its own special style, which may differ in each newspaper. Note too that headlines may use **pc** for brevity.

A billion is one thousand million (not a million million, as formerly).

See also under "Money".

Nuns / sisters

Most "nuns" should be called *sisters* (only those in solemn vows, like Benedictines, are *nuns*).

Nowadays sisters and nuns prefer to include their surnames – so not **Sister Agnes** but **Sister Agnes Smith**.

Members of religious orders and congregations usually have letters after their names to identify the order. Here are the principal female ones –

CHF	Holy Faith
CP	Cross & Passion
CSB	Brigidines
CSsT	Trinitarians
DC	Charity / V de Paul
FCJ	Faithful Companions of Jesus
FMM	Franciscan Missionaries of Mary
FMOL	Franciscan Missionaries of Our Lady
FSM	Franciscan Minoresses
IBVM	Loreto
LCM	Little Company of Mary
LSA	Little Sisters of Assumption
LSU	La Sainte Union
MMM	Medical Missionaries of Mary
MSHR	Missionary Sisters of Holy Rosary
OLC	Our Lady of Charity
OLSH	Our Lady of Sacred Heart
OP	Dominicans
OSA	Augustinians
OSB	Benedictines
OSC	Poor Clares
OSU	Ursuline
PBVM	Presentation
RCE	Religious of Christian Education

RGS	Good Shepherd
RJM	Jesus & Mary Sisters
RNDM	Notre Dame des Missions
RSC	Sisters of Charity
RSCJ	Sacred Heart Society
RSHM	S. Heart of Mary
RSM	Mercy
SCJ	Cluny
SHCJ	Holy Child
SJG	John of God
SM	Marists
SMA	Salesians
SPC	St Peter Claver
SSL	St Louis

See also under "Catholic Church titles".

OK

OK, not **okay**.

Only

Only goes immediately before the word it refers to. Eg –

> **He drinks only at weekends** (ie, at no other time).

> **He only drinks at weekends** (ie, he does nothing else).

Option

Option, not **alternative**, when there are more than two choices. **Alternative** means one of two –

He had three options (not **three alternatives**).

The word **choices** and **possibilities** are also acceptable.

Over

Over means **above**. It does not mean **more than**.

Wrong: **Over 20 members attended.**
Right: **More than 20 members attended.**

P

Peerage

If peer prefers to dispense with title, do so too. Otherwise use the title **Lord** for members of nobility below rank of duke. The further complications of titles are of little importance in Ireland, but can be checked in *Debrett's Peerage.*

Per cent

Per cent is two words and should be spelt out. So do not use **%**, **p.c.**, **pc**, or **percent**. However, **pc** is acceptable in heads, when space is at a premium, and also in tabular material.

Political affiliation

In political stories, put it in brackets after politicians' names, but only if relevant to the story. Eg –

Cllr Mary Smith (Lab)
John Smith, TD (FF),

Possessive

Possessives ending in **S** take a second **S**. Thus –

Dickens's novels
Dylan Thomas's poetry

But note that the latest issue of *Chambers's Dictionary* calls itself **Chambers' Dictionary**.

Exceptions:
1. When the following word starts with **s** –

For goodness' sake

2. When the possessive ends in an 'iz' sound –

Moses' law

Presbyterian Church titles

Title	First reference	Second reference
Minister	**Rev John Smith**	**Mr Smith**
Moderator of Presbytery and Synod	**Rev John Smith**	**Mr Smith**

Title	First reference	Second reference
Moderator of Assembly	**Rt Rev John Smith, Moderator of the Presbyterian Church**	**Mr Smith**

Press conference

Since the coming of the electronic media, the correct term is **news conference.** (However you still need a **press card** to get in!)

Public life titles

Position	First reference	Second reference
County councillor	**Cllr Mary Smith**	**Cllr Smith**
Alderman	**Alderman Mary Smith**	**Ald Smith**
Mayor	**The Lord Mayor of Dublin, Alderman Smith**	**The Lord Mayor** or **the Mayor**
Dail deputy	**Mr John Smith, TD** or **Mr John Smith, TD (FF Cavan-Monaghan)**	**Mr Smith** (or **Mrs/Miss/Ms**)
Senator	**Senator John Smith**	**Senator Smith**
Taoiseach	**The Taoiseach, Mr Smith**	**The Taoiseach** or **Mr Smith** (or **Mrs/Miss/Ms**)

Position	First reference	Second reference
Tánaiste	**The Tánaiste, Mr Smith**, or **Tánaiste John Smith**	**Mr Smith** or **the Tánaiste**
Party leader	**The Fianna Fail leader, Mr Smith**	**Mr Smith** (or **Mrs/Miss/Ms**)
Government minister	**The Minister for Finance, Mr Smith** or **Finance Minister John Smith**	**Mr Smith** or **the Minister**
Minister of state / Junior Minister	**The Minister of State for the Environment, Mr John Smith**, or **Junior Environment Minister John Smith**	**Mr Smith** or **the Minister**
Secretary of State for Northern Ireland	**The Northern Secretary, Mr Smith**	**Mr Smith**

Note 1: When a public title is foreign, this should be clearly indicated. It is incorrect to say **the Prime Minister, Mr Smith**. It should be **the British prime minister, Mr Smith**, or **British Prime Minister John Smith**.

Note 2: In first formal reference, a junior minister gets first name and surname, whereas a government minister gets only the surname. (In informal writing, however, both names are given.) See above examples.

Note 3: Opposition shadow posts in the Dail are lower case. Eg –

**Fine Gael's / Fianna Fail's / The PDs'
spokesperson on finance**

Q

Quotations

> **Basic Rule 1**: Always use double quote marks (" "), except – use single quote marks (1) for a quote within a quote, and (2) in headlines –

> **According to witness, his exact words were, "I will get you for that."**

> **"His exact words were, 'I will get you for that,' and I believed him," witness said.**

> **Basic Rule 2**: Only the exact words of speaker (or writer) should be inside the quote marks.

If you *add* words the speaker did not utter, put them in square brackets [ ].

If you *remove* words from the quote, replace them with three full points (**...**) – four, if a whole sentence was omitted. Thus –

> **"They have left us our ... dead, and ... Ireland unfree shall never [in our lifetime] be at peace."**

Titles of newspapers and magazines, and of books, plays, operas and ballets, are in italics, not in quotes. Titles of record albums are in italics, but the individual tracks are in quotes.

Position of punctuation marks in quotes:

At the end of a sentence, quote marks follow the comma or full point if the whole sentence was the quote –

> **"I want nothing from you."**
> **"I want nothing from you," she said.**

But, if only part of the sentence was the quote, quote marks precede the comma or full point –

> **He was nicknamed "the Towering**
> **Inferior".**

Exclamation and query marks follow the same guidelines –

> **"What do you want?" he asked.**
> **And who is "the Towering Inferior"?**

Colon and semi-colon always follow the final quote mark.

When a quotation runs for two or more paragraphs, put quote marks at start of each paragraph, but not at end of each. Only the final paragraph has closing quotes. Thus –

> **"Four score and seven years ago our**
> **fathers brought forth upon this**
> **continent a new nation.**
>
> **"Now we are engaged in a great civil**
> **war, testing whether that nation ... can**
> **long endure."**

Rather than have a number of paragraphs of quotation, it is better to sandwich direct and indirect quotation. This is particularly apt for interviews –

> **"I have always wanted to return to Ireland,"**
> **Mr Smith said.**
> **He recalled that he had always hated Irish**
> **weather, and even now was worried about it.**
> **"But I'm going to give it a fair try," he said.**

In fictional dialogue, create a new paragraph every time the speaker changes. Eg –

> **"I don't believe you," he said, reaching**
> **for the bottle to pour himself another drink.**
> **"Why not?"**
> **"Because you're a liar."**
> **Mary gasped. "How dare you!" she said,**
> **and slapped him hard across the face.**

Likewise, in cross-examination dialogue for a court report. Here, however, the quote marks can be dispensed with. Thus –

> **Mr Sullivan: Is it true you have been on**
> **the edge of serious crime for some years?**
> **Murphy: I suppose so.**
> **Mr Sullivan: And now you have crossed**
> **that divide?**
> **Murphy: Yes.**

Note 1: Most book publishers in Ireland and Britain differ from newspapers, in that they prefer single quote marks (whereas US publishers prefer doubles). Check the particular house style before writing.

Note 2: Some word processors (especially in newsrooms) now have keys for left-hand and right-hand quote marks (" ") as opposed to the old general-purpose quote marks (" "). These special keys should be preferred, and *must* be used if type is to be set directly from what you key in .

R

Race/colour/status

Race, colour or status (for example, **Asian**, **black**, or **traveller**) should be omitted unless strictly necessary to the story.

Ranks

See entries under "Air Corps", "Army", "Naval Service", "Garda".

Realise

Not **realize**. Likewise for similar words.

Religious orders/congregations (male)

Members of religious orders and congregations customarily have letters after their names which identify the order.

Here is a list of the male orders and congregations:

CB	John of God
CP	Passionists
CM	Vincentians
CSSp	Holy Ghost
CSSR	Redemptorists
IC	Rosminians
LC	Legionaries of Christ
MSC	Sacred Heart Missionaries
O Carm	Carmelites
OCSO	Cistercians

ODC	Discalced Carmelites
OFM	Franciscans
OFM Cap	Capuchins
OMI	Oblates
OP	Dominicans
O Praem	Norbertines
OSA	Augustinians
OSB	Benedictines
OS Cam	Camillans
OSM	Servites
SCA	Pallotines
SCJ	Sacred Heart Fathers
SDB	Salesians
SJ	Jesuits
SM	Marists
SMM	Montfort Fathers
SSC	Columban Missionaries
SSCC	Sacred Heart Community
SSP	St Paul's Society
SSS	Blessed Sacrament Fathers
SVD	Divine Word

Note 1: These letters do not take full points, and are placed between commas –

Father John Smith, SJ, will lecture on ...

Note 2: Priest-members of religious orders get title **Father**, not **Rev** (See under "Catholic Church titles").

For a listing of female orders and congregations, see under "Nuns/sisters".

Religious terms

Certain verbs are peculiar to religious functions. They should be used accurately. Here is a short list of preferred verbs:

Most denominations:
Sacraments are **administered**; prayers are **offered**; services are **held**; ministers and priests are **ordained**.

Catholic:
Mass is **celebrated**, **offered** or **sung** (not **said**); the Rosary is **recited** or **said**; services are **held**. A child is **baptised**, not **christened**. A priest is **ordained**; a bishop or archbishop is **consecrated**; a cardinal is **named** or **created**, then **receives the Red Hat**; a pope is **elected**, then **crowned**.

Church of Ireland:
Holy Communion is **celebrated**; Morning Prayer is **held** or **said**. A deacon is **made**; a minister is **ordained**; a rector is **instituted to a parish** (not **installed in a parish**). A bishop is **consecrated**, then **enthroned**.

Reported speech

Reported speech, especially in quotes, is not confined by the rules of any stylebook, since it is the utterance of persons who neither know nor care about stylebooks. It should be left as it is.

However, lapses of grammar or good taste in a person's speech may be corrected, especially if printing the lapse might cause embarrassment to the speaker, or bring the speaker into ridicule, or give the impression you were mocking the lapse.

Roads/motorways

Omit full points and dashes. Eg –

> **M50**
> **N11**
> **L3**
> **T55**

Robbery/house breaking/burglary/theft/stealing

Theft is the act of **stealing** (by stealth). **Robbery** is to deprive wrongfully and forcibly. **House breaking** is what it says. **Breaking and entering** is the same, but usually refers to commercial premises. When done at night it is **burglary.**

Romania

Romania, not **Roumania**.

S

Said

Said is the safest word. Beware of words that imply more, unless you intend such implication – eg, **admitted, conceded, agreed, alleged, recalled, insisted, asserted, declared, reminded, suggested, emphasised, stressed, hinted, claimed.**

Scots / Scottish / scotch / Scotsman

A person is a **Scot** or a **Scotsman** or **Scotswoman**. People are **Scots**. Everything about them is **Scottish** (eg, **The Scottish National Party**). A drink or a terrier is **scotch**.

Seasons

Seasons are written lower case. Say **autumn**, not **fall** (which is exclusively American).

Semicolon

Semicolon (;) is halfway between a comma and a full stop. Use as follows:

1. When a full point is too much. Eg –

   Caesar said: I came; I saw; I conquered.

2. When a comma is not enough. Eg –

   Also killed were Jane Eyre of Dublin;
   Jack Brown, a visitor from London;
   and three tourists from the US.

If only commas were used here, the visitor from London could be a different person from Jack Brown.

Note: Full sentences must be separated by at least a semicolon: a comma is not enough. Thus the following is wrong –

   Jim loved his mother, his wife
   couldn't stand her.

It should be –

   Jim loved his mother; his wife
   couldn't stand her.

Set

Avoid **set**, in expression of future, unless there is still some doubt. Otherwise it adds nothing to the meaning. Eg, do not say –

> **The Government is set to introduce legislation . . .**

Just say –

> **The Government is to introduce legislation . . .**

Sexist language

Sexist language is offensive, even when used inadvertently. We are expected to be sensitive. It is a matter, not of political correctness, but of courtesy and respect.

> **Basic Rule 1**: Pick a gender-free word, where there has been a tradition of defining male and female roles differently. Do so even when referring to males. Thus –

> **worker** (not **workman**)
> **photographer** or **camera operator** (not **cameraman**)
> **supervisor** or **overseer** (not **foreman**)
> **householder** or **home maker** (not **housewife**)
> **representative** (not **spokesman**)
> **adulthood** (not **manhood**)
> **garda** (not **ban garda**)

This means avoiding, where possible, words that end in **ess** –

> **authoress**
> **negress**
> **poetess**
> **murderess**

But **actress** and **hostess** are acceptable.

> **Basic Rule 2**: Male writers should avoid any expression that could be taken as patronising or demeaning to women, or that could imply that women are less competent. Thus avoid –

little lady	**your one**	**gal**
better half	**bird**	**young thing**
old dear	**little old lady**	**lady**
girl (when over 14)	**dame**	**mot**

> **Basic Rule 3**: In *news reports*, avoid reference to a woman's appearance or family circumstances (such as her number of children), if such reference would not be made about a man in the same situation.

So do not say –

> **President Robinson looked stunning**
> **in a blue outfit.**

unless you would likewise say –

> **The Taoiseach, Mr Reynolds, looked**
> **stunning in a grey suit.**

Do not use husband's first name for a woman (eg, **Mrs John Smith**).

For couples, write **John and Mary Smith**, without titles. Not **Mr and Mrs John Smith.** In society listings, write **the John and Mary Smiths**.

Plurals are usually more gender free than singulars. So a phrase like –

> **A person can make his contribution ...**

can become –

> **People can make their contributions ...**

See also "Gender-free expressions".

Shall / will

Modern Irish usage prefers **will** in most instances that occur in news stories.

Sic

When you use an unusual spelling, word, or expression, and you do not wish the subeditor to change or correct it, put the word **[sic]**, in square brackets, immediately after it. Eg –

> **"I regard him as a complete eejit [sic],"
> the witness said.**

Sir

Sir always takes the first or christian name, even in second reference. Eg –

>First reference: **Sir John Smith**
>Second reference: **Sir John** (not **Sir Smith**)

Slang

Slang should be avoided, except in reported speech. But see caution in "Reported speech" entry.

Square brackets [ ]

Square brackets are used to insert words inside a quotation, which the speaker or writer did not utter. Eg –

>**He said, "I love my country [Ireland] more than any other."**

T

Telephone numbers

Put area code in brackets. Thus –

>**(091) 24411**

If readers require fuller details, present them as follows –

Use **+** for international access code. Follow with country code; then area code (with only zero in brackets; then subscriber number. So the above Galway number would be –

+ 353 (0)91 24411

That

Omit after **said**, (unless context requires it). Eg –

> **He said he was tired.**

not

> **He said that he was tired.**

Time

Time is expressed thus: **4.45 p.m.** — **2.05 a.m.** — **3 p.m.** (not **3.00 p.m.**, as zeros here are redundant).

Note that **a.m.** and **p.m.** are lower case, and have full points.

Say **midday** or **noon** (not **12 noon**, which is redundant). Likewise for **midnight** –

> **Lunch is at noon.**
> **The bells will ring at midnight (June 3-4).**

Note: When writing **midnight**, it prevents confusion if you give the two dates, for before and after midnight (**June 3-4**).

In reporting spot news, time is often expressed as **early this afternoon**; **shortly after 4.30 a.m.** This is usually enough for the reader. However, when readers require the exact time, include it (eg, advance notice of a meeting).

Avoid redundancies like **11 a.m. this morning**. Instead, say either –

> **The meeting will take place at 11 this morning.**
>
> or
>
> **The meeting will be at 11 a.m. today.**

Note: **12.01 a.m.** refers to after midnight;
12.01 p.m. refers to afternoon.

Use of **o'clock** is colloquial. Confine it to reported speech, features and colour stories.

Time-span is expressed thus –

> **The sale of work is from 2 to 5 p.m.**
> (not **from 2-5p.m.**)
> **The seminar is from 10.30 a.m. to 5 p.m.**

Hyphenation is acceptable before the noun –

> **The 2-5p.m. period**

Present tense can often express a future event –

> **The draw takes place Sunday at 3 p.m.**
> **U2 start their world tour in July.**

Use present tense for any situation that is continuing –

> **The Taoiseach said yesterday he believes the Northern problem is soluble.**
>
> not
>
> **The Taoiseach said yesterday he believed the Northern problem was soluble** (has he changed his mind by today?).

Note: Some Irish journalists prefer the second of the above examples, we must in fairness point out. However, we recommend the first.

Use present tense for all headlines, unless the event happened in the past and is only being revealed now –

> **Letters reveal de Valera's thoughts**
> but
>
> **De Valera wanted papal approval, letters reveal**
>
> **Man punched wife, court told**

See also under "Day" and "Date".

Titles

Titles of newspapers, magazines, books, plays, music albums, are put in italics, NOT quotation marks. Individual book chapters, and tracks in an album, go in quotes. See also entries "Italics" and "Book references". Names of ships, aeroplanes, and buildings stay in roman type, without quotes.

Note 1: As a general rule, all words in a title are capitalised, except prepositions, conjunctions and articles (definite and indefinite). Eg –

> **How to Win Friends and Influence People**
>
> **Portrait of the Artist as a Young Man**

Whiskey / whisky

Whiskey is Irish. It is also american and Canadian. **Whisky** is Scotch.

Glossary

While the Rathmines Stylebook has been made as simple as possible, a few words may be unfamiliar to readers who are not journalists. They are explained here:

Abbreviation: Shortened form of a word. Eg, **Sept**. instead of **September**.

Acronym: A pronounceable word, that is in fact customarily pronounced, made from the initials of several words. Eg, **Aids** (Acquired Immuno-Deficiency Syndrome). But not **HIV**, which is pronounceable, but not usually pronounced.

Arabic numerals: 1, **2**, **3**, **4**, **5** – as opposed to *roman numerals* (**I**, **II**, **III**, **IV**, **V**).

Bold: Print that looks like this (often used for emphasis).

Capitalise: means to put the first letter of a word in capitals (Like This). If the whole word is to be in capitals (LIKE THIS), it is referred to as **all caps**). Capitals are also called **upper case**.

Catchline: The single word put at the top of a story to identify it.

Collective noun: A noun expressing a group. Eg, **herd** of cattle; **bunch** of grapes; **jury**; **team**; **government**.

Colour story: a descriptive piece of writing, often including atmosphere or people's feelings or reactions to an event, including those of the writer.

Common noun / **proper noun**: A *common noun* is a name that applies to all members in a class of things. Eg, **saint**; **county**; **tower**. A *proper noun* is the name of a particular one of them. Eg, **St Francis**; **Tipperary**; **Eiffel Tower**.

Copy: The written material a journalist produces for publication. When typed on paper, it is called *hard copy*; on a computer terminal or word-processor screen, or in a computer memory, it is called *electronic copy*.

En rule: Another name for a *dash*.

First reference/ second reference: *First reference* means the first time a person or thing is mentioned in a story. *Second reference* means the second and subsequent times the person or thing is mentioned.

Full point: Another word for *full stop*. Also called a *period*.

Gender: Connotation of male or female contained within a word. Eg, **actor/actress**.

Initial: The first letter of a word.

Initial cluster is made up of first letters of words. Eg – **RTE**; **JCB**; **EC**; **INTO**. If it can be pronounced as a word, and is customarily so pronounced, it is called an *acronym* (see above).

Italic: *Print that looks like this* (as opposed to roman, which is the more usual type, and looks like this).

Lower case means small letters as opposed to capital letters (like this as opposed to LIKE THIS).

Parentheses: Another word for *brackets*. The thing inside the brackets is called a *parenthesis*.

Quotes: Short for *quotation marks* (""). Also called *inverted commas* or *quote marks*, and used to indicate someone's actual words. To put something in quotes means to write it "like this".

Reported speech: The actual words spoken by a person. Placed between quotation marks.

Small caps: Capital letters that only come up to the level of a lower-case letter – LIKE THIS instead of LIKE THIS. They help to make initial clusters less obtrusive (eg, **John Smith, FRCSI**).

Spot news: An unplanned or unexpected event such as a fire, an accident or a crime. Eg – an air display at Baldonnel is *news*; a crash during the display is *spot news*.

Story: Any news report or feature.

Index

About the Author

In 1963 David Rice founded *Irish Spotlight*, the Dominican magazine which the *Evening Herald* described as "so outspoken and topical that every Sunday, daily, and evening newspaper in the country has quoted it." During the 1970s he was a newspaper journalist, editor, and syndicated columnist in the United States, and twice won the First Place award for columns at the National Journalists' Association (Sigma Delta Chi) annual awards in Seattle. His column also won the Washington Newspaper Publishers' Association First Place award. Rice returned to Ireland in 1980 to lecture at the Rathmines School of Journalism. In 1987 he travelled 38,000 miles around the world to research his book *Shattered Vows*, which went to No. 1 on the hardback bestseller list. It was filmed for Channel 4 as *Priests of Passion*. In 1989 he was invited to Beijing to train journalists for the Chinese government's news agency, *Xin Hua*, and reported for RTE on the Tiananmen Square massacre. He later returned to China and secretly interviewed 400 young Chinese, for his book *The Dragon's Brood: Conversations with Young Chinese*. He has a major new novel, *When the Moon Was Blood*, being published in spring 1994 by Blackstaff Press. He continues to lecture in Practical Journalism at Rathmines.